new Baby,
new Life

"A refreshing book brimming with relatable personal anecdotes and practical advice on enjoying life's simple pleasures, practising self-compassion and creating a more nurturing environment for our children."

— **Carmen Lee**
Behavioural Insights practitioner | Mother of one

"Whether you are a new parent or not so new parent, you can find simple and easy ways to bring joy into your day with this book. Using experiences from her own life, supported with research evidence, Sabrina shares with readers pieces of her joyful life to nudge you to find your own."

— **Dr Leung Chi Ching**
Psychologist | Mother of two

"Three words to describe this book. Relatable, enjoyable and applicable."

— **Melvin and Geradine**
Parents of a 9-month-old bambino, Ian

new Baby, new Life

Finding Joy and Applying Behavioural Science in Your Daily Life

SABRINA NG

Candid Creation Publishing

Candid Creation Publishing books are available through most major bookstores in Singapore. For bulk order of our books at special quantity discounts, please email us at enquiry@candidcreation.com.

NEW BABY, NEW LIFE
Finding Joy and Applying Behavioural Science in Your Daily Life

Author:	Sabrina Ng
Publisher:	Phoon Kok Hwa
Editor:	Zoe Toh
Page Layout:	Geelyn Lim
Cover Illustration:	Sabrina Ng
Cover Design:	Ryanne Ng
Published by:	Candid Creation Publishing LLP
	167 Jalan Bukit Merah
	#05-12 Connection One Tower 4
	Singapore 150167
Website:	www.candidcreation.com
Email:	enquiry@candidcreation.com
Facebook:	www.facebook.com/CandidCreationPublishing
ISBN:	978-981-17560-0-9

National Library Board, Singapore Cataloguing in Publication Data
Name(s): Ng, Sabrina.
Title: New baby, new life : finding joy and applying behavioural science in your daily life / Sabrina Ng.
Description: Singapore : Candid Creation Publishing LLP, 2024.
Identifier(s): ISBN 978-981-17560-0-9 (paperback)
Subject(s): LCSH: Parenting. | Parenthood.
Classification: DDC 649.1--dc23

For my newly completed family, you are much loved!

For all new parents out there, you are not alone.
If you have been mentioned in this book
(I would have told you so), know that I was thinking of you and
that you have inspired me in its writing.

Special shout-out to my ex-teammates, including the alumni,
for sharing your personal applications, which I have incorporated.
To my wonderful ex-boss and mentor Dr Lal Nelson, thank you
for bringing me into the world of behavioural science.

Our Lives Regressed

Our lives regressed—
The sleepless nights
Our home, cluttered with toys
Once again, we had to feed, bathe and clothe someone
Our travels, no longer carefree.

But why does life feel so content
Our hearts, so full
To hear the pitter patter of your footsteps
See your toothy grin
And have you in our arms, the meaty, bouncy you.

You have changed our lives so much
Even if we were complaining (it's probably momentary)
Your brothers adore you
And you love to hang out with them as if there is no age difference
You occupied our hearts quickly, as if you have always been here.

Thank you, Cheng
For the privilege of being your parents
For bringing us immense joy
For teaching your brothers responsibility and love for a younger sibling
For being you.

We love you
More than words
Can ever say.

- Mum, with love

Contents

Foreword

I was intrigued when Sabrina told me that she had written a book. For nearly one decade, I taught behavioural science courses at the Yale-NUS College. As the lead behavioural scientist at the Ministry of Home Affairs, Sabrina often visited the college as a guest lecturer. Each time, I'd marvel when she described how her team applied behavioural sciences to improve MHA's work.

In *New Baby, New Life*, Sabrina put aside her usual focus on safety and security to tackle her biggest challenge yet: Being a mother of three. Parents of newborn children often find a mismatch between the idyllic portrayals of parenthood and the reality of sleepless nights. In this book, Sabrina shares her journey to "hack" parenthood by applying behavioural science.

In the first half of the book, Sabrina reviews the science of well-being. She describes how tweaks to the environment or everyday activities can spark joy through the application of scientific knowledge. In the second half of the book, Sabrina describes how behavioural science can help everyone to implement plans and stick to them. She even anticipates potential obstacles and tells you how to overcome them.

It is often said that doctors make the worst patients and that experts rarely practise what they preach.

However, this book is a testament to how Sabrina puts into practice the knowledge she has always espoused in her professional life. As a reader, be prepared to hear the forefront of scientific studies translated into everyday practical tips. This is paired with Sabrina's personal accounts—like how she tried to keep plants alive to increase the greenery in her house.

New Baby, New Life is a highly approachable book with bite-size tips for the busy 21st century life. I read the book in one go and took notes of the different ideas I wanted to try in my life. I'm sure my fellow readers will do the same.

In whatever stage of life you find yourself in, may you read this book and level up your happiness!

Dr Jean Liu

Director, Centre for Evidence and Implementation

Founder, Insights Bridge Consultancy

Hello! It's great to have you here. I want to begin by explaining how this book came to be.

My third child Zander was born in July 2022 and we got promoted to a family of five. Passersby who see us like to chuckle and point out that we have three boys. Gender aside, we also get some attention because my older children, Zach and Zaden, are much older than the baby, being 11 and eight years older than him respectively—hence the title of this book, *New Baby, New Life*.

Your life will certainly change with the welcoming of a new child and ours did get a major upheaval with this one! Not only for us parents, it's a whole new life for the children as well, now that they have a new baby brother. Their lives have changed overall as we regrouped as a family of five. Thinking back, our lives were relatively easy pre-Zander as we could sleep through the night, the children could handle themselves and travelling was a breeze as we could go anywhere without worrying about flight time and whether the destination is child friendly.

Prior to my pregnancy, I was already working on a well-being book based on behavioural science concepts. I decided to tweak the focus of the book to emphasise on well-being following the birth of a new child as it puts many of the concepts to use and to the test as well. I wrote a substantial part of this book during my maternity leave while experiencing the changes and challenges, and at the same time constantly reflecting on how I could do better to manage the situation at home with what I knew from work. Without this new baby and new life, this book may never have been completed!

If I were asked to explain concisely what this book is about, it's about how we can tackle things when the days seem overwhelming in this new life and how knowledge from behavioural science can help. This makes up the two main parts of the book in that order, but feel free to check out the sections in any order that you like. I hope that this will help you in your own journey. Know that your struggles are not yours alone and hopefully, we can emerge as stronger and happier mums and dads.

Having worked in the area of behavioural science in the Singapore public service for the past 11 years, my personal research interests have been in applying behavioural science to improve well-being and extending it to the home. It is my sincere hope that the research and tips mentioned in this book are both interesting and useful for you.

Congratulations and let's do this together!

Throwback to the initial days after Zander was born: I'd been excited about the maternity leave and started the leave with what was on hindsight an unrealistic dose of optimism. I had hazy recollections of my maternity leave in the past and vaguely remember even managing to enjoy the second one (I last took maternity leave close to 10 years ago!). I imagined that this would be a time of rest and family bonding because I wouldn't have to work. It would be a somewhat surreal time— like a sabbatical—during which, apart from taking care of a new baby I could also learn new things and find time to do what I enjoy.

Fast forward three weeks into my confinement period and I already felt that things were going awry. Somehow, I must have forgotten how difficult this period was—not different from how people say women tend to discount the pain of childbirth after. The constraints on my behaviour were challenging although I wouldn't say I was that compliant to start with. The confinement food got tiring. The nagging from various parties, albeit for my own good, was on the brink of becoming unbearable. Instead of feeling taken care of, I felt physically and mentally bound.

Not surprisingly, the unforgiving round-the-clock feeding schedule took a toll. But what really affected me was the inability to regulate my mood, especially when dealing with my older children. It was always tiring to tutor them after work, but it seemed even more so during my maternity leave, although I was not working! They wanted to be where the baby was, including during feeding, but I saw it as a form of distraction and even annoyance, rather than a gesture of love for their baby brother. I often hurried them to bed and rushed them to fall asleep fast "as the baby is waking up soon for a feed". I would often shout at them impatiently and feel super lousy afterwards. I was not on top of the situation at all and it was frustrating.

With a new kid on board, whether the child is your first, second or more, your life is definitely going to be shaken up. You would probably have anticipated this when you were expecting, but it will be most keenly felt now after the birth of the baby. Your responsibilities, priorities and routine will get a major update. You will probably struggle, not only with managing the newborn, but also with your older children (if any), the other people in your life and also yourself. While the addition of a new child will most certainly bring tremendous joy, seasoned parents know that it also comes with its necessary challenges and sacrifices. This was an old-but-gold advice given by a buddy when my eldest was born.

In this din, it is not uncommon to spend each day in a whirl just settling the essential stuff. There is hardly any mind space to consider other things, let alone to think about self-care. You probably heard of the phrase "happy wife, happy life". In the same vein, happy mums and dads are essential for a happy home and happy children. Only when we take care of ourselves can we then be in the right frame of mind to give the best care to our children.

As mentioned in the Preface, the first part of this book will focus on our mental well-being, specifically self-care in the context of limited time, attention and sleep. (I wrote this while recalling a close colleague who used to down three cups of coffee in a workday and still felt extremely sleepy when his second was born.) This means you won't be reading about fancy, time-consuming self-care ideas, but how you can care for yourself with what you can find in everyday life. This refers to the simpler pleasures in life, instead of the big things. Do not discount the impact of small joys though. Small things add up. Knowing how to find enjoyment and contentment in our daily life does help to make us a happier person overall. American polymath Benjamin Franklin couldn't have put it more aptly when he said, "Happiness consists more in small conveniences or pleasures that occur every day, than in great pieces of good fortune that happen, but seldom to a man in the course of his life." Slowly but surely, we will feel supported and uplifted by these small yet significant pockets of happiness.

This book covers the strategies for finding happiness and contentment in everyday life, as well as utilising behavioural science to improve our lives as follows:

- **Part 1: The Science of Spotting Joy**

  Learn how to be in a generally positive state of mind through strategies for finding happiness and contentment in everyday life.

- **Part 2: Applying Behavioural Science to Our Personal Lives**

  Learn specific tips on how behavioural science can be applied to improve our daily lives. Our emotions, the dynamics in the home and our children's behaviour may all be different in this "new life". I have organised the tips according to these key categories so that it may be easier for you to relate to and apply them.

- **Part 3: Case Studies: Real-life Applications**

  Take a look at how behavioural science is being adopted and actively applied in real-life situations ranging from teaching a toddler the alphabets to setting reminders to cancel a subscription plan.

The Science of
Spotting Joy

PART 1

Joyspotting

I first read about "joyspotting" in one of my favourite magazines *Flow*. The term, coined by American designer Ingrid Fetell Lee, involves being aware of the elements in our environment that bring us joy and to consciously surround ourselves with them[1]. Lee differentiated this sense of joyfulness from happiness, which is more durable and experienced as a calmer state of mind; and also from pleasure which, in her view, goes deeper. In Lee's words, joyfulness is the spontaneous smile on one's face when in contact with something that brings joy.

Sources of joy can include places or things, people or animals, colours or shapes. Lee identified a number of aesthetic features that tended to bring joy. She noted that not everyone is attracted to the same aesthetics and one's preferences can also vary, based on needs and the situation. Some examples include:

- Bright colours, because of their energising factor
- Things with festive character, e.g., birthday cakes, fireworks, pinatas
- Views which are associated with a sense of freedom, e.g., a rolling stretch of lawn or a large body of water
- Blooming flowers, as they signify a new start
- "Magical" phenomena like the Northern Lights and stars

- Round shapes, due to the association with imagery from our childhood, e.g., bubbles, balls, balloons, etc.
- The sight of abundance, e.g., in candy stores and flea markets

Lee was of the view that once we know how to spot joy, we would be able to find joyfulness everywhere. We would then want to take note of them so that we can experience the same joy over and over again. In psychological terms, this works when we "remind" our System 2 to alert us when a moment of joy happens. Psychologists Kahneman and Tversky refer to System 2 as our slower and more reflective way of thinking, as opposed to System 1, which is fast, unconscious and intuitive[2]. We can tap on System 2 by making a mental note to be alerted to things that give us a spontaneous moment of joy when we sense the ends of our mouth curling up, i.e., we smiled. Otherwise, it is easy to leave such moments in our subconscious and not remember them.

One of my sister's key sources of joy is good food— it is quite easy to keep her happy—while a dear friend's sources of joy are her dogs and road trips to Malaysia with her husband. Sources of joy need not be from the outside environment. They can include things that we can spot even when being cooped up at home. In sharing my sources of joy, I am hoping that some of my simple pleasures will overlap with yours as a form of prompting what may bring joy to you. However, it is most certain that you and I will differ in many of our preferences, as noted by Lee. Hence, it is imperative that you learn how to spot your own joy. You will notice that I have deliberately left out children as a source of joy as I would be referring more to sources that can be found in the environment. To ensure that we do not forget these moments, Lee suggested making a note of them by keeping a joy journal (see page 8 for reference).

---

[1] Leclaire, Annemiek. "Happy to Be Here". *Flow*, Mar 2020, pp. 13-20.

[2] Kahneman, Daniel. *Thinking, Fast and Slow*. Penguin Books, 2011.

Savouring

Closely related to the concept of joyspotting is "savouring", a term coined by social psychologist Fred Branyt in 2021, which refers to the deliberate effort of fully enjoying a positive moment and making the feelings last[1]. People who consciously find ways to make the most out of happy experiences have been found to be more satisfied with life, are more optimistic and are also less likely to be depressed.

To savour, we first need to be keenly aware of what makes us happy, i.e., joyspotting! When we are able to spot joy, we can then savour using a number of techniques:

- **Savouring the present.** Once you spot something that makes you happy, mentally hold on to the moment to extend it and remind yourself to be grateful for such small but precious moments in your life.
- **Capitalising on the present.** To savour even more, you can share the positive experience with others, e.g., taking a photograph and sharing it. People tend to respond in kind to expressions of positive emotions (think back on the last time you shared something happy with your friends and how they responded), which has the effect of extending the positive experience.
- **Savouring the past.** This refers to thinking back on a happy event and trying to recreate the positive

emotions felt at that time. Pay attention to how the emotions make you feel and let them linger until you are ready to go back to whatever you were doing.

On reflection, my usual method of savouring is probably by sharing the experience with like-minded friends or by taking photographs! I have noticed what makes me happy (all the more important in this trying period) and have tried to make the most of it, and I hope that you will be able to do so too!

---

[1] Davis, Tchiki. "What is Savoring – and Why Is It the Key to Happiness?". *Psychology Today*, 3 Jul 2018, www.psychology today.com/sg/blog/click-here-happiness/201807/what-is-savoring-and-why-is-it-the-key-happiness?amp.

My Joyful Home

Close friends who have been to my place probably know that I love my home. It is neither fancy nor big and is almost always very messy somewhere, but I love it. The best part is, there are so many spaces that I love in the house: The balcony, the "planty window" by our dining area, our artsy study, the beautiful photo wall my husband put up in the living room when we rejuvenated the house a few years back, etc. What this means in joyspotting talk is that it would be easy to find joy in so many different areas just in my house alone!

Indeed, the first places I visit every morning after waking up are my planty window and balcony. I would spend a few moments immersing myself in the sights and sounds, checking out the new leaves, buds and blooms, if any, and do a bit of tidying up. Then, I'll feel ready to move on to the rest of my day. This brief ritual, which does not take much time at all, helps me start my day on a calm and joyful note. When I work from home in my study and I get tired or need a mental break, I'd just have to turn around and admire the mini art pieces. The art wall in my study brings me so much joy.

Yes, I have chosen to start my joy journal with my first joy being the home! It probably makes the most sense to do so since a home is such an important construct. We spend much of our time at home (even more so for new parents), but more importantly, home is where we return to after a tiring day. It is a place where we rest and recharge; it is where we can and should truly be ourselves. It is where our children grow, and family and close friends gather. Home is indeed where the heart is! How our home is shaped therefore has a profound impact on our happiness and well-being.

To understand the qualities of a happy home, architectural and design firm Resi conducted a "Science of a Happy Home" study in 2020 by surveying 4,000 UK residents on what constitutes a happy home for them. This study was most recently reconducted in 2023[1]. The latest study found that the six qualities of a happy home, uncovered in the 2020 study, were still relevant:

1. **Providing security and stability.** The home needs to meet our basic need of being a safe and stable shelter. Hence, renters tend to feel less secure about their homes.

2. **Whether the home is "nourishing".** This refers to homes that optimise light, sound and ventilation. The view is important: People were happier with their homes when they were happy with what they could see from their windows.

3. **Adaptability.** This looks at whether the uses and functions of the spaces in the home can be easily adapted to meet new needs. Those who were most happy with their home felt that their home met their needs.

4. **Whether the home is relaxing.** Those most satisfied with their home said that their home always or often makes them feel relaxed. In terms of which spaces are the most important (for relaxation), people often cited their living room and bedroom. In the latest survey, those who described their

homes as organised were also more likely to be happy at home.

5. **Connectedness.** Those who described their home as "sociable", i.e., being a comfortable space to facilitate connection with family, friends, etc., were more likely to be happy at home. Many also wanted a connection to nature in the home.

6. **Whether it mirrors who we are.** Not surprisingly, the research also found that those most happy at home said that their homes reflect who they are, e.g., in terms of values or personality. Pride in the home is also important. The vast majority of the happiest homeowners said that they were proud of their homes most of the time.

Knowing the above, it is no wonder that I love my home. I love the view from our balcony (in fact, it was one of the key reasons we bought this house), it is cosy and inviting—although it could be tidier—and importantly, it also reflects our taste and preferences, and incorporates a lot of what we love. I do feel proud of our home!

Before you start to wonder why I am sharing these with you when I said this book will cover easy self-care ideas, I want to clarify that I am not asking you to do a huge revamp of your house and definitely not now! But if we know the common qualities of a happy home, we may be able to make small tweaks to make it one that facilitates joyspotting and happiness. For example, can we draw attention to the lovely sunset view we have from the kitchen window? Can we reorganise parts of the home slowly so that there is less clutter? Can we put up some décor that reflects our style and preferences? We can learn from the Danes, known to be one of the happiest people in the world, on how we can transform our home into a hygge headquarters!

Homes as hygge headquarters

Pronounced "hoo-ga", the word *hygge* originated from a Norwegian word meaning well-being. For the Danes, hygge is about creating an atmosphere or an experience which makes them feel safe, loved, at home and consequently, contented and happy[2]. The Happiness Research Institute in Denmark believes that hygge is a key ingredient in the Danish recipe for happiness. When asked where they experience the most hygge, 71 per cent of the Danes said it is at home. I cannot agree more and I cannot think of any place that would be more *hyggeligt* than our own home. Here are some manageable ways to achieve hygge at home:

- **Making an area of the home slightly cosier.** Tips include making a cosy nook where we can snuggle up with the baby (and on a good day, with a book and a hot drink), incorporating warm lighting and also nature, which can refer to plants, as well as furniture made from natural materials like wood.
- **Something as simple as hot drinks.** Yes, you read it right! When asked what they most associate with

hygge, 86 per cent of the Danes mentioned hot drinks, which topped the scale. Beverages of choice included tea, hot chocolate, mulled wine, etc., but the one that came up tops—to no surprise—was coffee. In Denmark, it is easy to spot the compound word kaffehygge, which means coffee and hygge.

- **Candles.** According to the European Candle Association (I never knew such an organisation existed!), each Dane burns six kilograms of candles each year. Twenty-eight per cent of Danes light candles every day: 23 per cent 4-6 days per week, 23 per cent 1-3 days per week. Candles are lit not only in the home, but in classrooms, boardrooms and offices. An essential part of Danish life, candles are said to provide a kind of emotional cosiness and happiness. This is another tip that is easy to follow.
- **Something sinful, like cake.** Hygge is also about giving oneself a treat once in a while. Hence, cakes are hyggeligt and so are chocolates. Hygge is, however, not about being fancy or extravagant. It is thus okay to indulge ourselves once in a while with a treat of our liking.

Reframing how we think about our home

Given the pandemic, most of us would have been cooped up at home for an extended amount of time until recent years. We would also have worked from home a lot more as many workplaces transited to a hybrid working arrangement. While many welcomed the hybrid way of working, me included, it is true that the lines between work and personal life have blurred. We seem to be working more hours when working from home, e.g., during lunchtime. We also have to manage the children when they are home, which can be a good or bad thing. This situation is exacerbated for new mums and dads, for we would definitely have to stay home a lot more with an infant in the house! If not managed carefully, this could lead to an increased sense of frustration and unhappiness.

Counsellor Ama Clarke, in her article "Home", urged people to reframe how they think about their homes[3]. Although a home is a confined space, she was of the view that we should not think of our home as just the four walls. Rather, it is about the feeling it gives us and the ways it nurtures us. Home can be the comfort our sofa provides at the end of a weary day, the enjoyment of a drink in our favourite mug, the embrace of our children or the soothing sight of our plants. With a mindful appreciation of our home, we can find joy in the simple but precious pleasures of our home, which can hopefully help to alleviate the feeling of being confined.

Wouldn't it be great if our home is a constant source of joy for us? With it being such an important part of our lives and our happiness, it is worth considering how to make the space welcoming, comforting and nurturing for each family member. Does everyone have their own favourite space(s)? Even without making changes, you can also start to discover what brings you joy in your own home using joyspotting.

---

[1] "The Science of a Happy Home in 2023". *Resi*, 21 May 2024, resi.co.uk/happy_homes_report.

[2] Wiking, Meik. *The Little Book of Hygge: Danish Secrets to Happy Living*. HarperCollins, 2016.

[3] "Home". *Counselling Directory*, 22 May 2024, www.counselling-directory.org.uk/memberarticles/home.

Rainy Days

"Oh, look! It's our favourite kind of day!"

No matter how busy the day or what has happened, rainy days never fail to lift my spirits. I feel instantly relaxed, calm, even uplifted at the sight of grey skies and feeling the comfortable, cooling weather on my skin. There is even the scent of rain that I recognise and like, although I have never been able to put it into words.

Prior to researching for this book, I had never thought of finding out why I had these positive feelings towards rain, but now I know! Apparently, enough people thought about this to conduct research studies and here's what they say:

- The pitter-patter of raindrops is a form of what scientists call "pink noise"[1]. Pink noise consists of all the frequencies we can hear, with the energy of the sound signal being more intense at lower frequencies, creating a deep sound. We are relaxed as our brain processes it as a calming, non-threatening noise[2]. Rainy days are great for our sleep as well, since our brain continues to process sounds as we sleep and noises can affect our rest. Pink noise has been found to slow down brain activity and improve the quality of sleep, which is why the sound of raindrops is often used in sleep-inducing relaxation music.

- A 2016 study on the role of odour-evoked memory found that memories evoked by odour are more vivid and emotional than those triggered by our other senses[3]. Medical Director Bryan Bruno, at Midcity TMS, New York, posited that the sweet, subtle fragrance of rain may have reminded us of enjoyable moments spent on past rainy days. This is known as the petrichor effect where the scent created by rainfall on dry soil has been said to trigger good memories, emotions and even nostalgia in some people, positively impacting their mood[4].

- Some people felt that being at home during stormy weather reminded them of how lucky they were to have warm shelter. It made them feel contented and prompted them to want to curl up on a sofa and enjoy the moment.

Did you also know that there is a word to describe lovers of rain? Pluviophiles are people who find joy and peace of mind during rainy days. I am undoubtedly a pluviophile!

When I asked my children why they like it when it rains, Zach said it is because it is dark and he likes it to be dark. I guess it somehow corroborates with the research on rain putting people in a wound-down, relaxed mode. Zaden loves how cool it is when it rains and he also likes to see the raindrops falling. The sight and sound of rain is really quite pleasant and therapeutic! Our lovely niece Charlene, likes rainy days as well. She loves the pitter-patter and the calming sight of rain, and rainy, cool nights are her absolute favourite!

Needless to say, the Z Bros used to be so excited whenever we were outside on a rainy day because they had the rare opportunity to jump around with their cool, kid-size umbrellas! Those were the days. I'd like to share with you our version of the rain song before I end this segment:

Rain, rain don't go away
You can also come again another day
Little Zander wants to play
Rain, rain don't go away

We are all made different. Some of us like the rain more than others. Rainy days are free for all so if you are not averse to rain and have not paused to enjoy what it has to offer, please do!

---

[1] "What is Pink Noise and How Does It Compare with Other Sonic Hues?". *Heathline*, 18 Apr 2023, www.healthline.com/health/pink-noise-sleep#does-it-work.

[2] "How the Sound of Rain Can Calm an Anxious Mind". *Heathline*, 20 Dec 2023, www.healthline.com/health/mental-health/rain-calms-anxiety#Negative-ions.

[3] Herz, Rachel. "The role of odor-evoked memory in psychological and Physiological Health" *Brain Sciences*, vol. 6, no. 3, 19 July 2016, p. 22, doi.org/10.3390/brainsci6030022.

[4] "4 Health Benefits of Walking in the Rain, According to Experts". *Verywellheath*, 23 May 2024, www.verywellhealth.com/health-benefits-of-walking-in-the-rain-8635150.

Growing Joy

Check out this really funny definition of a "crazy plant lady" I found online:

"A wonderful lady who has an addiction to plants, a woman who finds great joy in buying more plants than she can handle or her space allows, a person who prefers the company of shaggy green foliage to people."

As much as I am a pluviophile, I am admittedly also a crazy plant lady. The first two sentences in the description above are true for me—I do have a plant obsession and I cannot quite resist buying interesting and beautiful plants. The third, not so, as I am quite sociable and I do like the company of humans quite a bit!

My green fingers might have been inherited from my parents as they both like to grow things and do so with much success and interest. For me, I have always relished the idea of having a nice little garden in my modest balcony. I just love having a space to hang out amidst nature within the home. How it nourishes my soul! My plants are indeed a huge source of joy for me.

Despite having green fingers, you can consider me to be a late bloomer in this regard. I have always liked plants, but did not always know how to care for them and keep them alive. I did not think of understanding their needs and we hardly have plants in the home after a while. That was, until the pandemic.

There was a huge houseplant craze during the days of the pandemic when we were all cooped up at home. I was one of those who reconnected with plants during that period. What did plants have to offer during those times? Why do plants make people happy?

- **Plants stimulate feelings of escape.** A study investigating the impact of greenery on mental health during the COVID-19 quarantine found that participants who experienced greenery indoors either by having houseplants in the home or having a view of greenery from inside the home, experienced significantly fewer symptoms of depression and anxiety, purportedly due to feelings of "being away" even when isolated[1].

- **Plants have a restorative capacity.** Assistant Professor of Horticultural Science Knuth at North Carolina State University posited that nature can recharge us. Seeing a plant when we are tired and mentally fatigued can provide a spark of interest, redirect our attention and help restore our mental and physical resources[2].

- **Plants help with self-care.** Known as "vitamin G" (with "G" referring to green), exposure to nature and greenery purportedly helps us feel relaxed and calm, improving our mood[3]. A systematic review of 50 empirical studies investigating the psychological benefits of indoor plants found that rooms with plants were perceived to be more comfortable, bringing about positive emotions such as calmness, peacefulness, cheerfulness, etc[4]. This applies even where there were very few plants, e.g., even where there is only one pot. In another experiment investigating the effect of indoor plants on comfort, researchers found that participants were most satisfied with green plants as compared to tinted or multi-coloured plants, plants with a slight scent as compared to those with strong or no scent, and preferred smaller to larger plants[5].

- **Plants can help reduce physiological and psychological stress.** A study involving young male adults assigned to either a plant task or a computer-based task found that those who were assigned to repotting a houseplant reported feeling comfortable and soothed, while those who were assigned a computer-based task did not[6]. Notably, the participants' blood pressure was measured as well, with the plant group registering a drop in their blood pressure while those assigned to the computer task saw a spike in theirs. Interestingly, even looking at pictures of plants have been shown to lower stress levels. Researchers exposed patients in a hospital waiting room to a plant, a poster of a plant or no nature and found those exposed to plant-related conditions reporting lower levels of stress[7].

It is probably not good enough to tell you how awesome plants are without sharing with you how to care for them. Being a serial plant killer does not make you happier around plants. Having lost and found the ability to keep plants alive, here are my three most important tips:

1. **You need to understand the plant you want to get.** Here is where I put my research experience to good use. I'll be sure to Google the plant, understand its origins and thus understand its needs—how much light and how much water. There are plants that need full sun, e.g., many flowering plants, and many others that do best under shelter by a brightly lit window. There are almost no plants that love low

light (except marimo moss balls which originate from the rivers and lakes, and are technically spherical-shaped algae and not moss), although some can survive under such conditions. In terms of watering, there are plants that are extremely thirsty, and others that can go for weeks without water. It is extremely important to know what the plant needs to survive and thrive in your care.

2. **You need to put it in the right spot.** Based on what you understand about the plant's requirements for light, you will then need to find the right spot for it in your home. If it needs full sun, it means that it must be put in a place where sunlight is shining directly upon it at least for a few hours a day. If it needs bright, indirect light, which is the case for many houseplants, it would be okay to place it by a window. Do note that our eyes are not good at discerning whether the lighting conditions are sufficient, i.e., it always seems to be bright enough according to what we see, but it is helpful to know that the intensity of light drops significantly every step away from the window.

3. **You need to feed it right.** This primarily refers to the amount of water to feed the plant, which can certainly make or break your human-plant relationship. It is generally safer to feed less than more for most plants, with the exception of the very thirsty ones. It is also very important to use pots that have drainage holes at the bottom, so that any

excess water can drip through to mitigate root rot. For those of you who want to help your plants grow even better, you can even consider feeding them with plant fertilisers once or twice a month.

Even during my pregnancy and after the baby's birth during the confinement period, I never stopped caring for my plants. I recall watering all the plants just before I had to check in to the hospital, planning to do so again when I return three days later. This was only possible because I never saw watering as a chore. In fact, I feel happy and even slightly excited when it is time to water them. I would also take the chance to scrutinise every plant for new developments.

Favourite view of my balcony garden.

If you already have plants and have been caring for
them yourself, you probably know how helpful they
can be in times of difficulty, without me telling you!
If you can, continue to take care of them and they will
in turn take care of you. If you don't have plants,
you may think that now is not the time to start, but
remember what the research says about not needing
to have that many, because even one will do?
Who knows, you may be starting a new journey with
a plant friend (and more) that has no looking back!

1 Dzhambov, Angel M., et al. "Does greenery experienced indoors and outdoors provide an escape and support mental health during the COVID-19 quarantine?" *Environmental Research*, vol. 196, May 2021, p. 110420, doi.org/10.1016/j.envres.2020.110420.

2 "What Science Tells Us About the Mood-boosting Effects of Indoor Plants". *The Washington Post*, 20 Apr 2023, www.washingtonpost.com/wellness/2022/06/06/how-houseplants-can-boost-your-mood.

3 Leclaire, Annemiek. "Happy to Be Here". *Flow*, Mar 2020, pp. 13-20.

4 Han, Ke-Tsung, and Li-Wen Ruan. "Effects of indoor plants on self-reported perceptions: A systemic review." *Sustainability*, vol. 11, no. 16, 20 Aug. 2019, p. 4506, doi.org/10.3390/su11164506.

5 Qin, Jun, et al. "The effect of indoor plants on human comfort." *Indoor and Built Environment*, vol. 23, no. 5, 22 Apr. 2013, pp. 709–723, doi.org/10.1177/1420326x13481372.

6 Lee, Min-sun, et al. "Interaction with indoor plants may reduce psychological and physiological stress by suppressing autonomic nervous system activity in young adults: A randomized crossover study." *Journal of Physiological Anthropology*, vol. 34, no. 1, 28 Apr. 2015, doi.org/10.1186/s40101-015-0060-8.

7 Beukeboom, Camiel J., et al. "Stress-reducing effects of real and artificial nature in a hospital waiting room." *The Journal of Alternative and Complementary Medicine*, vol. 18, no. 4, Apr. 2012, pp. 329–333, doi.org/10.1089/acm.2011.0488.

Flowers

Before I got into the houseplant craze, I used to buy cut blooms from the supermarket to make a vase bouquet. Its beauty, though delicate and fleeting, was a feast for my eyes and soul. After becoming a crazy plant lady, I told my husband that I didn't need cut flowers anymore because I have nature all around! On reflection, I wonder if that is really true because I do feel something different around flowers.

It sounds like common sense that people (okay, specifically women) like flowers, but you may be surprised to know that it has been scientifically proven that flowers do make people happy. In a 2005 study, researchers sent out three different gifts—a candle, a fruit and sweets basket or a mixed-flower bouquet—

to 147 women who agreed to participate in a study about "normal daily moods". The couriers, who were actually observers, took note of each participant's facial expression as they received the gift[1]. The study found that all of those who got the flowers unanimously exhibited what psychologists call a Duchenne smile, i.e., a smile involving not only one's facial muscles, but also the muscles around the eyes, hypothesised to represent a genuine indicator of true enjoyment. Three days later, the flower group was also found to report more positive moods than their candle and fruit basket counterparts. The researchers posited that flowers could be rewarding to humans because of the sensory stimuli they provide, i.e., their symmetry, colour and fragrance. The universal symbolic meanings of flowers may have also led to a positive learned response. Similarly, the act of giving flowers symbolises love and appreciation for the recipient and thoughtfulness of the giver, which evokes positive emotions and happiness.

The research team, interestingly also sought to test if flowers had an impact on men. In this second study involving "random" gifts that people may receive in an elevator, researchers found that, contrary to cultural expectation, men were also significantly more likely to display a Duchenne smile when presented with a flower as compared to when they received a non-floral gift like a pen.

The following happy brain chemicals have been found to be triggered by flowers[2]:

- **Dopamine.** Flowers have traditionally marked the coming of abundance after a hungry winter. Although people have abundance of food all year round now and no longer associate flowers with food, our brains may still be hardwired to see flowers as a reward, releasing dopamine, which is known as the feel-good neurotransmitter.
- **Oxytocin.** When flowers are given or received, oxytocin, often called the bonding hormone, is released, thereby creating a warm feeling of togetherness. Flowers communicate the intention to invest effort in a relationship. Its fragility also serves as a reminder that relationships need care and effort to maintain.
- **Serotonin.** Growing flowers causes serotonin to be released as it stimulates a sense of pride and competence.

A solution to having flowers and also keeping them for longer might be to keep flowering plants ourselves! If the conditions are right, we may see the plant flower again and again. As we do not have direct sun in the house for much of the year, most flowering plants are out of the question for me except for one species—hoyas! Somehow, they have been the most accommodating and have been generous enough to bloom again and again by my dining area window. Their waxy flowers usually bloom in a cluster (called an umbel), which is a really pretty and dainty sight. I am always very excited to see new flower buds forming from the peduncle (stalk from which the inflorescence form) and feel very happy when they develop into mature flowers (serotonin released!). If you want a starter flowering plant that is forgiving and easy to manage, consider hoyas! Choose one which already has peduncles as they will keep budding and blooming from these same spots.

I guess what I am saying in this segment is, do indulge
yourself in flowers if you also enjoy them and need
a quick perk-me-up! (Husbands, get the hint or wives,
try gifting your husbands flowers since the research
shows that men also react positively to them.)
They don't have to be expensive and just one stalk
will do (similar to the idea of having just
one potted plant). You can make that one plant
a hoya and enjoy its lovely flowers as well!

---

[1] Haviland-Jones, Jeannette, et al. "An environmental approach to positive emotion: Flowers." *Evolutionary Psychology*, vol. 3, no. 1, 1 Jan. 2005, p. 147470490500300, doi.org/10.1177/147470490500300109.

[2] Breuning, Loretta G., "Why flowers make us happy". *Psychology Today*, 6 Feb 2023, www.psychologytoday.com/sg/blog/your-neurochemical-self/201706/why-flowers-make-us-happy?amp.

Joyful Colours

"Red, orange, yellow, green, blue, indigo
And violet are the colours of the rainbow
Colours are everywhere you see, and
Colours were made for you and me
La la la la la la la la la la la
Everywhere you go, everywhere you see
Colours make the world a beautiful place to be."

This song stuck with me throughout the years, although I probably last sung it to the kids when they were toddlers and I have not sung it to the youngest yet.

And yes, this is a segment on the lovely thing we call rainbow. Why are rainbows featured in dreamy songs or whimsical birthday cakes and why do they always come to mind when we think of objects that represent cheer or happiness? Why do they stop people in their tracks and who later on plaster photographs of rainbows all over social media platforms?

According to a BBC Culture article, colourful images of hand-painted rainbows, started in Italy, appeared in windows across the world in a unanimous movement of solidarity during the time of COVID-19 lockdowns in Europe[1]. Why do rainbows bring hope? What's their deal?

The science: National Geographic defined a rainbow as a multicoloured arc created when sunlight strikes water droplets. The light entering a water droplet is refracted, then reflected by the back of the droplet, then refracted again at multiple angles as it leaves the droplet, causing the light to separate into its component colours to create the beautiful optical illusion we know as a rainbow[2]. It is perhaps no surprise that rainbows have been a symbol of hope in many cultures because they appear magically after a storm, signifying a beautiful, fresh start. Like a rainbow after the rain, the handmade rainbows speak of hope for a brighter future once the current circumstance passes. More reasons why rainbows bring cheer and happiness:

- Research suggests that colours can affect our mood. We all have natural associations and preferences to colour. Because rainbows are made up of cheerful, vibrant colours, we are naturally drawn to them.

Bright colours also make our surroundings feel alive, energising us.

- When asked why they were happy to see a rainbow, some said that rainbows are special because they are rare, unexpected and fleeting. It is indeed human nature to be drawn to things which are rare and which do not last for a long time (and are therefore seen to be more precious). This is known as the scarcity bias!

I would love to be able to catch rainbows too, though I usually get to see them only through other people's photographs because I am usually not lucky enough to spot them. However, ever since I discovered suncatcher stickers, I have been able to create beautiful and strong rainbows in my own home on sunny days when the stickers catch the sunlight. Although the rainbows are no longer rare nor fleeting, I am still very happy to see them every time! I think rainbows bring joy and hope whether they are manmade or not.

Beautiful man-made rainbows.

Beautiful man-made rainbows.

Take a moment to marvel at the fleeting beauty
of a rainbow the next time you spot one! If you would like
to bring instant cheer to your home, you can consider
using suncatcher stickers. Watch the lovely rainbows
adorn the interior of your home and notice
how you instantly feel more cheerful.
This is a happiness quick fix that does not require
any time on your part at all, once the stickers have been
affixed! It is a wonderful décor idea for a nursery too!

---

[1] Vince, Gaia. "Rainbows as signs of thank you, hope and solidarity". *BBC*, 18 Apr 2023, www.bbc.com/culture/article/20200409-rainbows-as-signs-of-thank-you-hope-and-solidarity.

[2] Jeannie, Evers. "Rainbow". *National Geographic*, 30 Apr 2023, education.nationalgeographic.org/resource/rainbow.

Making Art

How can we have some fun while being cooped up at home? The easy answer to this question for me is to make art!

I have always enjoyed making art. It probably started when my mum gave me my first craft kit when I was in primary school. I did not quite understand what to do then and don't recall there being any instructions. My mum was equally clueless as she is not crafty by any measure. When I got older, I realised that that was a cross-stitch kit, but instead of crosses, I had sewn vertical lines.

By the time I was in secondary school, I had become quite the crafter. I tried lots of different crafts and cherished all the instruction sheets that accompanied the kits. In fact, they are kept in a huge plastic file to this day and stored in my craft cupboard. I have never once thought of discarding them.

My love for making art remained strong to this day. I also thoroughly enjoy hanging out with two girlfriends with whom I share a strong interest in crafts with. We would dabble in various kinds of art and spend quality time doing what we all enjoy most when we meet up. What a treat!

You would also have seen that I have shared snippets of my art with you throughout this book, although my art is by no means professional. I have also just picked up watercolour painting not so long ago, self-learning through books and online tutorials, so I am by all standards an amateur! I hope that you will enjoy the mini paintings anyway.

There has been a lot of research on how art—both partaking in and observing it—improves our mental wellbeing:

- **Dabbling in art lowers our stress levels.** Using cortisol (via saliva samples) as a biological indicator of stress levels, a number of studies have found that subjects involved in an art activity have lower measured levels of cortisol post-activity, regardless whether the activity was pre-defined[1]. For example, in a 2016 study, students, staff and faculty members of Drexel University were given 45 minutes of art making time and were allowed to choose from a variety of materials to do so (collage materials, clay, markers, etc.). They could create any art piece they wanted and were told that there was no expectation of the final artwork. The results showed that cortisol levels were lowered for approximately 75 per cent of the sample group. There was also a statistically significant drop in the mean cortisol levels overall[2]. When asked how they felt about the experience, subjects reported that they found the session to be relaxing and enjoyable, allowing them to lose track of time. Some also said that the session evoked a desire in them to make art in the future. Importantly, there were no significant differences in the results between experienced and non-experienced artists, suggesting that one does not have to be good at art to enjoy the related rewards.

- **It feels good to make or view art.** Making art is intrinsically rewarding. It allows people to express themselves and their feelings, which in turn boosts their self-esteem and confidence. Even viewing art activates our brain regions, which are related to reward. An avant-garde project by Art Fund, the UK's national fundraising charity for art, used technology to allow visitors to see the impact of art on themselves. Using a specially designed headset, visitors can see their brainwaves real-time on screen as they admire pieces of art[3]. The images show that when visitors view something that they find beautiful, their brain's pleasure centres light up and its visual sensory centre is engaged more intensely. This is purportedly due to the release of dopamine.

- **Indulging in art allows people to focus on the moment.** Psychologist Mihaly Csikszentmihalyi suggested that people can experience a state called "flow" when they are making art. When in a state of flow, one can become completely immersed in what they are doing, losing track of time and even not noticing that they are hungry or tired[4]. Art allows people to temporarily escape the busyness of everyday life and is also a great way to digital detox. Csikszentmihalyi further suggested that the benefits of being "in the zone" stretch beyond the experience itself. It is associated with subjective well-being, satisfaction with life and a general sense of happiness.

- **Art can also help in care and treatment.** As it could be challenging for people to articulate the difficulties they face with their illness, art provides an alternative and non-threatening solution to express one's emotions. Research has shown that making art provides hope, self-confidence and a sense of control to patients, alleviating feelings they may have, such as anxiety, depression and stress[5].

How about art in coffee, i.e., latte art? Does it bring you joy? Personally, I seek out and really appreciate coffee places with beautiful latte art and tend to be disappointed with the lack of. Literally turning a cup of coffee into a work of art, latte art's intricate details and visual appeal, whether it is a simple heart, leaf, smiley face or a more sophisticated swan, elevates the experience and makes the coffee-drinking experience so much more joyful and photo-warranting! Most of us probably can't enjoy latte art at home (I tried to persuade my husband to learn to no avail) so it would have to wait till we go out!

Favourite pieces of self-made art.

Although making art is an enjoyable experience for me,
not everyone thinks that they are cut out for art.
Positive psychologists have also suggested that activities
are most likely to improve our well-being where there is
person-activity fit, i.e., where the activity is well-matched to
our personality. If you are not adverse to art and have
pockets of time to spare, you can consider taking some
time to make art (remember, you do not have to be good
in art to enjoy its benefits). It is also a great idea to partake
in small art projects with your older kids as part of
spending quality time with them. It is a win-win outcome
if you are like me who loves art and has a child who
values quality time a lot! And yes, it is also okay to sneak
in a cup of latte art coffee when the day calls for it.

---

[1] Kaimal, Girija, et al. "Reduction of Cortisol Levels and Participants' Responses Following Art Making." *Art Therapy*, vol. 33, no. 2, 2 Apr. 2016, pp. 74–80, doi.org/10.1080/07421656.2016.1166832.

[2] Gharib, Malaka. "Feeling Artsy? Here's How Making Art Helps Your Brain". *NPR*, 13 Jun 2024, www.npr.org/sections/health-shots/2020/01/11/795010044/feeling-artsy-heres-how-making-art-helps-your-brain.

[3] Villa-Clarke, Angelina. "The Feel Good Factor: Why Art is a Dopamine Hit for Travellers". *Forbes*, 13 Jun 2024, www.forbes.com/sites/angelinavillaclarke/2024/02/16/the-feel-good-factor-why-art-is-a-dopamine-hit-for-travellers.

[4] Robb, Alice. "The 'Flow State': Where Creative Work Thrives". *BBC*, 13 Feb 2024, https://www.bbc.com/worklife/article/20190204-how-to-find-your-flow-state-to-be-peak-creative.

[5] Ilkay, Keser. "The Use of Art in the Care and Treatment of Chronic Diseases". *ResearchGate*, 14 Jun 2024, www.researchgate.net/publication/312939858_The_Use_of_Art_in_the_Care_and_Treatment_of_Chronic_Diseases.

Joy in Music

Do you like to listen to music? What's your happy song?

I wish I can understand why my eldest son needs to be plugged in to music all the time, even when he is doing his homework or revising for a test. Personally, I do enjoy listening to music, but probably not when I am trying to read or understand something.

That said, most of us will probably agree that listening to music that we enjoy can enhance our mood. There is strong backing from the research on the benefits of listening to music we like (note that listening to music we do not like can have the opposite effect)[1]:

- **Music and relaxation.** Listening to relaxing music positively impacts our automatic nervous system by slowing our breathing, regulating our heart rate, lowering our blood pressure and reducing muscle tension.

- **Lifting our spirits and reducing our stress levels.** Music energises us and stimulates feelings of enjoyment by increasing the production of adrenaline and the reward hormone dopamine, and reducing levels of the stress hormone cortisol.
- **It can strengthen our immune system.** Music was also found to increase the production of salivary immunoglobulin A, an antibody responsible for strengthening the immune system.

Our body moves as a reflex when we listen to music, creating a sense of enjoyment. In 2009, a team of researchers from the Institute for Psychology at the Hungarian Academy of Sciences, together with the Institute for Logic, Language and Computation at the University of Amsterdam, measured 14 sleeping newborn babies' electrical brain responses to sound by playing versions of a rock drum rhythm that played throughout or skipped a sound[2]. They found that where a missed note broke the rhythm, the babies had a brain response indicating that their expectation of the next beat was not met (which shows that they can sense a rhythm and know when to expect the next beat). This ability to detect the beat in music is known as "beat induction". Fun fact: Beat induction is considered to be uniquely human. Even our closest evolutionary relatives, the chimpanzees, do not move to beats!

Another interesting 2023 study conducted by fat-free yogurt brand Müllerlight and music psychologist Dr Michael Bonshor, sought to unveil the formula for the happiest song ever. The survey, conducted on 2,000 UK respondents, saw 71 per cent of respondents saying that music is their greatest mood booster, taking an average of 14 seconds to make them feel happier. Of the respondents, 64 per cent said they listen to music to cheer themselves up, most often when they are lonely, sad or when it is cold and dark outside. Based on songs respondents reported to be happy, the researchers found the formula for the happiest song:

Major key + 137 BPM + 7th chords + strong beat + 4 beats in every bar + short intro + (verse + chorus)^2 + repeated riffs + high volume + bright tone + (predictability*surprise).

In layman terms, the happiest songs are in a major key, have approximately 137 beats per minute, include "7th chords" (i.e., where the seventh note of the scale is added to the main three notes of the chord to create interest) and a strong 1-2-1-2 beat to them so that people can dance along to. These songs also kick off with a bang straight away (with a short introduction), are played in high volume and have notes played in a bright and bouncy way by lively instruments, such as electric guitars. They also typically end with a repetitive rhythm or guitar riff (i.e., incorporating a repeated sequence of notes or chords, making the song all the more memorable). According to the formula, these were the top 10 scientifically happy songs:

1. Good Vibrations by The Beach Boys
2. I Got You (I Feel Good) by James Brown
3. House of Fun by Madness
4. Get the Party Started by P!nk
5. Uptown Girl by Billy Joel
6. Sun Is Shining by Bob Marley
7. I Get Around by The Beach Boys
8. YMCA by Village People
9. Waterloo by ABBA
10. September by Earth, Wind & Fire

Now I know why I enjoy Korean drama original soundtracks (OSTs) so much! While I do not know Korean or music well enough to know if they use the same formula, the ones I love sure are bright, bouncy, catchy and cheery. I always sneak in a song or two when I have the chance and dance along!

> If you need a self-care quick fix, tune in to
> your favourite music, even if it is just for a short while
> (remember, 14 seconds will do).

---

[1] Bonshor, Micheal. "Happy Songs: These Are The Musical Elements That Make Us Feel Good". *Neuroscience News.com*, 2 Jan 2024, neurosciencenews.com/music-happiness-22910/.

[2] Honing, Henkjan. "Do Newborn Infants Have a Sense of Rhythm?". *Psychology Today*, 6 Aug 2023, www.psychologytoday.com/us/blog/music-matters/200901/do-newborn-infants-have-sense-rhythm?amp.

Chocolates

There was ONE little treat that I insisted on having during my confinement, which comforted me much—chocolates! Yes, I secretly ate chocolates at the risk of being nagged to death by the confinement lady. It was one of the few things I took that provided me with some semblance of normal life.

While I have always liked chocolates, I did not think much about how eating chocolates could perk up my day and give that small but important sense of comfort during trying times. Why do chocolates make us happy?

In a number of studies conducted around the world, eating four to five moderate portions of chocolate a week has been associated with higher rates of happiness. This is purportedly due to the pleasure-inducing compounds found in chocolate[1]:

- **Tryptophan.** An amino acid found in small quantities in chocolate that is used by the brain to make serotonin, a neurotransmitter that can produce feelings of happiness.
- **Phenylethylamine.** A chemical which promotes feelings of attraction, excitement and nervousness associated with the initial euphoria of falling in love. This chemical also acts as an anti-depressant by combining with dopamine that is naturally present in the brain.
- **Theobromine.** A weak stimulant that works alongside caffeine to produce the "high" that many people experience after getting their chocolate fix.

Given that the above compounds are only present in small amounts in chocolate and are likely to be almost entirely digested before they reach the brain, some scientists suggested that the happiness effect caused by consuming chocolates could perhaps be psychological. In other words, it could be the experience of eating chocolates, thus satisfying a food craving, that releases endorphins, leading to happy feelings.

One more reason to eat chocolate: Scientists have found that dark chocolate, in particular, is beneficial to our health. The higher cocoa content in dark chocolate provides high concentrations of an antioxidant called flavonoid, which reportedly prevents cancers, protects blood vessels, promotes cardiac health and counteracts high blood pressure.

This is another self-care quick fix that is really easy to do! You do not need to feel guilty about indulging in chocolates once in a while.

____

[1] "Does Chocolate Make You Happy?". *BBC Science Focus*, 6 Jun 2023, www.sciencefocus.com/the-human-body/does-chocolate-make-you-happy.

Sleep When the Baby Sleeps

I want to add this short note about sleeping when the baby sleeps because it is such a common piece of advice given by the confinement lady or well-meaning visitors. However, while the advice was probably given with the new mother's welfare in mind, I'd like to argue that its practicality is questionable. I did not quite understand how we could (literally) sleep like a baby. Perhaps it is possible for those with only one baby, but what if you had more children? Wouldn't they need some time with you? Also, wouldn't it be quite a waste spending a whole month just feeding, eating and sleeping? Are there not things that we would want to do to lift our spirits or make us more relaxed?

May I suggest that instead of sleeping when the baby sleeps, we sleep when we need to (we all know to do this without people telling us!) and rest when the baby sleeps? This refers specifically to mental rest: Finding some time to indulge in any of your joys, like those in my joyspotting journal, for a needed perk-me-up. It could be to listen to your favourite music, drink your favourite beverage or do a quick activity that you enjoy. Akin to power naps, such power mini happiness sessions serve to relax and rejuvenate us in between caring for the new baby and fuel the way ahead till it is time for the next pit stop.

Special Note for Relatives and Friends

A friend shared a post on Facebook that really resonated with me: *Hold the Mother, Not the Baby* by writer and eating disorder advocate Danielle Sherman-Lazar. The post spoke of showing concern, support and love for the new mother, not just the baby. The baby is, of course, important. No one needs to be told how precious the baby is and that is why the baby is already adored by everyone. But the new mother, who may still be healing, who very likely is still struggling and who may be experiencing a whirlpool of emotions, deserves some love too. Sherman-Lazar called for relatives and friends to, instead of saying, "I'm coming to see the baby," to say instead, "I am coming to see you and meet the baby too," because the mother is probably the one that needs to be held more.

Hold the Mother, Not the Baby

Because the baby's being taken care of—
fed, snuggled, and given all the love in the world—
by not only the mother,
but her partner, grandparents, siblings, cousins,
and friends.

But the mother,
may have gaps in her mind from lack of sleep,
may be mechanical in her motions as she's healing,

may feel more like a mess than a mother,
may be sitting in bed, crying, feeling overwhelmed in
her body and life,
may be full of mum guilt because in her mind, she's not
good enough,
and she's bleeding, wincing in pain, swollen
and emotional.

And the mother's that baby's whole world and needs to
be seen, so she doesn't disappear into that
postpartum fog.
So, hold the mother, not the baby.

A mother agrees that her baby matters more.
But she's hurting, while she's the person behind the baby,
in the background, making it all happen:
feeding her baby at all hours,
snuggling her baby close to comfort newborn cries,
and being that baby's everything.

So, it's the mother who needs your love.
And a mother will remember who held her up.

So instead of "I'm coming to see the baby",
try saying, "I'm coming to see you and meet
the baby, too."
Because the mother needs to be held more.

After I read the above post for the first time, our 14-year-old niece came to visit and she was excited to see the baby. She asked how often does he feed and was told that he wakes up every two to three hours. Before she went home, she hugged me and told me, "It must be hard for you to take care of the baby because he wakes up every two hours." The coincidence was uncanny, but it was the sweetest thing I heard and it deeply touched my heart. Thank you, Bella.

Applying
Behavioural
Science to Our
Personal
Lives

What is Behavioural Science?

Behavioural science is simply defined as the science of understanding and influencing human behaviour. A relatively new field of study and cross-disciplinary in nature, it draws insights from disciplines, such as economics, psychology, neuroscience and sociology. Behavioural science also takes an empirical focus, putting many of the insights to the test in the lab and the field.

There are countless ways that behavioural science can be used in our personal lives and using it to merely achieve work-related outcomes would be such a waste! As I understood more about its application in the context of work, I was also actively thinking of how it could be used to improve life at home—to better manage the children, myself, the home, etc. In this section, you will find a collection of behaviourally-informed tips and tips from related fields that have been useful for me and a number of my teammates. I hope that you will find them helpful.

The opposite of joyspotting

While joyspotting aims to help us identify the things that make us happy so that we may immerse ourselves in them, the opposite of trying to put a finger on the things that make us unhappy is probably also very important to do.

Why? This is so that we may be more aware of our triggers and hopefully be more prepared to manage them. It is not a good idea to get upset over the same things again and again, with no plans for improvement. For myself, even though I adore my kids, I am aware that I am often frustrated and harsh when coaching them on their schoolwork. Over time, such angsty study sessions which were meant to be for their benefit, would only serve to hurt our relationship.

After we are aware of what makes us unhappy, particularly for situations that tend to repeat themselves or are quite unavoidable, it is then helpful to find a way to better manage our emotions. One way to do this is to use the implementation intentions strategy devised by psychologist Peter Gollwitzer. This involves making a plan for how we will react when a particular situation arises[1]. If-then plans typically take the following format:

"If <u>a situation arises</u>, then I will <u>respond in this way</u>."

Such plans help us react to a particular situation in a pre-specified way by making the opportunity to act mentally salient so that it can be identified easily. Formulating a specific response ahead of time also means that we are automatically prompted to respond according to plan when the moment calls for it. If-then plans are one of the best validated plans for bridging the intention-action gap, i.e., the gap between the intention to do something and actually performing the behaviour. They have been found to be effective in promoting goal pursuit, managing distractions and temptations, deterring undesired social influence and dealing with emotions, as in this case. When one makes such a plan ahead of time, he or she is also prompted to think about when and how to carry out a specific action, and the plan also acts as a form of commitment for following through.

For my being-triggered-when-coaching-the-kids scenario, my if-then plan would be: "If I feel frustrated with the kids regarding their schoolwork, then I will take a brief timeout till I feel calm again."

I had originally just asked for myself to be calm while still seated at the table with them, but it was very challenging! I figured later that it is better to just take a timeout for a mental break (as well, an opportunity for them to escape from scary mummy for a while).

Even if we did not manage to use the plan every time—for instance, somehow the intention did not translate to action that day—managing to use it sometimes is still better than never. What should we do if we feel that we messed up? If you feel bad about it and think you could have managed the situation better, there is really no shame in apologising to the kids even, although they may be eight and you are 38. Children do appreciate it when parents acknowledge that they could also do better sometimes.

Do make a list of your triggers and see whether you
are able to make if-then plans to deal with them.
For me, I am sure that I can find a few more.

---

[1] Gollwitzer, Peter M. "Implementation intentions: Strong effects of simple plans." *American Psychologist*, vol. 54, no. 7, 1999, pp. 493–503, doi. org/10.1037//0003-066x.54.7.493.

Tapping on Our Fresh Start

Changing ourselves is difficult to do. For those of you who, like me, finds it hard to make a change and needs some anchor from which to effect change, you can consider tapping on the fresh start effect.

The fresh start effect is a psychological phenomenon that refers to the tendency for people to perceive temporal landmarks, such as the start of a new year, new month, birthdays, holidays, etc., as opportunities to start afresh and make positive changes in their lives[1]. A 2014 study focusing on the effect found that Google searches for the term "diet" increased significantly following the start of a new calendar cycle, with the greatest interest in dieting observed at the start of a new year (i.e., new year resolutions), followed by a new week and a new month. In the second part of the study involving students and their gym attendance, researchers likewise found that gym attendance increased at the start of a new year, month and week, and that students also exercised more at the start of a new semester and also on the first day following a school break. They were also found to exercise more frequently right after their birthdays!

Researchers posited that such temporal landmarks demarcate the passage of time, creating new mental accounting periods which stimulated the feeling of a fresh start. Past imperfections are left behind and the person is motivated to pursue aspirational behaviours.

Apart from time, significant moments of change, such as moving house, getting married or having a new child, also stimulate feelings of a fresh start and present timely opportunities for behavioural change. Sometimes, a new purchase can stimulate the fresh start effect as well—a friend at work bought a new pair of running shoes and feels motivated to pursue a new running target!

Since new parents would naturally be in the position of a fresh start, perhaps we could ride on the fresh start effect and consider what we may want to do differently hereon: It could be to lead a healthier lifestyle, be more prudent with our money, or simply to live each day more mindfully (admittedly, I need to get better at all three!). If you are considering using if-then plans from the previous chapter and need some motivation to get started, consider coupling them with the fresh start effect (e.g., the new school semester) to get rolling!

---

[1] Dai, Hengchen, et al. "The fresh start effect: Temporal landmarks motivate aspirational behavior." *PsycEXTRA Dataset*, 2013, doi.org/10.1037/ e513702014-058.

Mindful (Not Mindfull) Around the Baby

Have you heard of the term "mindfulness"? Mayo Clinic defines mindfulness as being attentive to the present, where we focus on being intensely aware of what we are sensing and feeling in the moment, without interpretation or judgment[1]. It often involves breathing methods, guided imagery and other practices to gently train the mind to settle into the present moment with the intention of improving our quality of life.

Studied in many clinical trials, practising mindfulness, often through meditation, has been found to be effective for alleviating conditions, such as stress, anxiety, depression and insomnia. Mindfulness applied outside of the clinical setting involves slowing down and deliberately focusing on how our body is feeling, from our breathing, our emotions, to our senses (e.g., listening intently to someone who is talking to us). When we sense that our mind is wandering, we need to bring it back immediately to what we were trying to focus on. This deliberate direction of attention is called monitoring.

Proponents of mindfulness say that being attentive to the present allows people to feel happier because it helps them take notice of the good things around them and better appreciate them. Some examples include enjoying the sights, scents and sounds in your garden, feeling the breeze on your skin on a rainy day and listening intently to the cute voice of your child. While this doesn't sound that hard to do, we are admittedly often "mindfull" instead of mindful. There is "noise" all around us and so many things are competing for our attention at any one time (for example, your children and spouse trying to speak to you at the same time). We are almost always multitasking. No one thing seems to be able to capture our undivided attention anymore.

How about the baby? Is he or she getting your undivided attention? To be honest, I heard about mindfulness years back, but have never taken it seriously, in part due to the perception of there being a lack of application. However, it recently struck me that I am not mindful even in the presence of my baby. I would play with him for a bit, then pick up my phone and start checking my social media, WhatsApp, etc. Repeat. My interactions with him have not been purposeful. Conversely, I realised that if I were mindful, the experience would be so different. I would probably notice how tiny and smooth his hands are, how nicely warm they are, and enjoy his little (okay, not so little) grasps on my hands. His toothy grin is so goofy it never fails to melt my heart. It is hard to explain how special such moments feel. You have to mindfully experience them for yourself.

I think it is also important to be mindful around the baby because he or she does not have that many distractions (yet) and does not have a phone. The baby would probably be looking at us and other members of the family all the time, waiting for someone to take notice of and to engage him (this is the case with our baby!). Because the rest of us are always looking at our mobile phones or the television, he sometimes gets upset and recently, even he is interested in the phone. He keeps wanting to grab it and has even learnt how to swipe it. It is indeed a wake-up call to reflect on our behaviour!

If you recall, the first section on joyspotting was about being aware of the elements in our environment that bring us joy. If we are mindful, we would also be able to better pick up the moments in our everyday life that make our day better, even if just for a bit. Surely, the moments with the baby are in this list!

---

[1] "Mayo Mindfulness: Practicing Mindfulness Exercises". *Mayo Clinic*, 10 Oct 2023, newsnetwork.mayoclinic.org/discussion/mayo-mindfulness-practicing-mindfulness-exercises/.

How Does Loving Our Children Look Like As They Grow?

If you have more than one child, you would probably have realised that it is quite a different thing to show your love to a baby or toddler vs. a tween or teenager. A baby wants his milk promptly, loads of attention and basically does not want you to leave his side. You are his food source, his source of comfort, his world.

A tween, on the other hand, is quite different. Take for instance, my second son Zaden. He is happy to chill out on his own when he wants to (especially when playing Roblox or watching YouTube), but he loves to cuddle and still says his "I love you's". He loves our attention, especially when it is one-to-one. He is also always very happy when I make the effort to pick him up from school or when we buy him his favourite food as he is a fussy eater. That said, he is also growing up. He recently said, "Mummy is being overprotective," when I repeatedly asked him to be careful as he jumped around the drain while we were walking along the road.

Dealing with the soon-to-be teenager is undoubtedly the most challenging. I think that maybe he himself and us parents are both not quite sure what we want the other party to do. He definitely wants a lot of space and freedom, and suddenly requires significantly less attention. He was especially chatty when he was younger, but now he is chattier with his friends. When he wants to share though, we have to give him our undivided attention. Loving him, from his perspective, may be to give him the autonomy he wants, yet be there for him where needed. Love certainly does not look the same with my different-stage children!

We know from research that it is important to customise our messaging to our target audience as people are more likely to pay attention when a message is relevant to them, due in part to the salience bias and also because we all have limited attention span[1]. In the same vein, our love needs to be personalised to the ones we want to show love to. It is no use insisting to love someone the way we want to when it is neither understood nor appreciated. Hence, aside from age-appropriate love, it is also very important to speak to our children in their own love language(s).

The concept is not foreign. Most of us would have heard of Dr Gary Chapman's "The 5 Love Languages". Essentially, it is about the five ways that people receive and express love, namely through words of affirmation, quality time, acts of service, receiving gifts and physical touch[2]. Dr Chapman argued that people communicate and prefer to receive love in different ways, and that understanding and speaking our loved ones' primary love language(s) can fill up their love tank when communicating our love in ways best understood by them. His later books, *The 5 Love Languages of Children* and *The 5 Love Languages of Teenagers*, similarly seek to help parents discover their child's love language and speak it.

It doesn't take rocket science to figure out the primary love language of my eldest. He is definitely the-way-to-his-heart-is-through-his-stomach kind of guy, i.e., act of service by feeding him good food (potential daughters-in-law, don't say I didn't share this greatest tip!). He also shows his love by making the family breakfast and snacks occasionally. That is why when I was working from home, no matter how busy I was, I tried my best to prepare bentos for him whenever he has Co-Curricular Activities (CCA) on Mondays. Although he looked rather cool about it, I know that he was actually very pleased with this gesture and also happy about being able to flex to his friends.

How about my second son? How many times has he asked us to go on night walks with him or play Beyblade together? He is undoubtedly a "quality time" type of guy. I am guilty of not spending enough quality time with him though—always asking him to wait or having him share the time with his brothers. This is the hard truth of having siblings, but I should really try harder! (Sorry, my darling!)

As for the baby, I am not certain what his primary love language(s) are yet—he is a little young to tell. Preliminarily, it seems to be linked to food too, like his eldest brother, as he is a foodie. It might also be "words of affirmation" as well, considering how pleased he is to get praises ("Handsome boy!") and also how we must always clap when he does something good!

Consider personalising your love to your child in terms
of age and also their love language(s). Although it may
not be easy to come to terms with the fact that the way
we love them needs to change (especially when it involves
backing off, asking fewer questions, trying not to
intervene so much for the older children),
making this change is probably inevitable.
To ensure that our love is effectively communicated,
felt and accepted, our best bet is to identify and
speak to them in their love language(s).

---

[1] "Why do we focus on items or information that are more prominent and ignore those that are not?". *The Decision Lab*, 29 Jun 2023, thedecisionlab.com/biases/salience-bias.

[2] Chapman, Gary D. *The 5 Love Languages*. Northfield Publishing, 2014.

The Important Nine Minutes of a Kid's Day

I cannot remember where I first read this, but I found the following insights by neuroscientist and psychologist Dr Jaak Panksepp really helpful! It is about the three key moments of our kid's day (roughly three minutes each), why they are important and how to spend these moments well[1]. The three moments are:

- When they wake up
- When they return from school
- Just before bed

Dr Panksepp argued that these moments are very important because they are when our kids are most impressionable and therefore how we interact with them in these daily short-but-crucial nine minutes can leave a lasting impact on them and our relationship. This is akin to what it means in behavioural science work to "make it timely", i.e., to intervene at the right time when people are likely to be the most receptive, for maximum effect[2]. The earlier example of leveraging key "moments of change" is also an example of a timely intervention!

Suggestions from the literature on how to spend these moments intentionally and positively:

- **When they wake up.** This is a difficult time for most parents, getting the kids out of bed, rushing them to get ready for school and shoving them out of the door. It was suggested that it is still possible to spend the time calmly, for example waking up slightly earlier for a quick breakfast together or to try to wake the kids up more gently (vs. shouting). The objective is to help the kids start the day on a positive note because no one likes to get shouted at the moment they wake up. How about with the baby? I think it is also a great idea to give the baby a loving cuddle and kiss when he or she wakes up, to show that we are elated to see him or her every time and that he or she is deeply loved. Such simple, consistent, yet powerful expressions of love can go a long way in building a strong, loving bond between you and your baby.

- **When they return from school, this being the longest period of separation from you.** This is an important time because the kids have just spent an entire morning or day at school and much could have happened, e.g., it could have been a great day or otherwise. While we may be very keen to know how their day went, the research suggested that we avoid bombarding them with questions. Instead, offer a cuddle and a snack to allow our children to relax and slowly open up about their day. When they are ready to share, we should try to listen to them. Essentially, we want our kids to feel welcomed, understood and valued. Thinking back on how my kids typically behaved after returning from school, I realised that they often cannot wait to share about the key things that happened, often shouting over each other in an attempt to share first. On reflection, I did not always listen patiently to what they had to say, sometimes rushing them to eat their lunch so I could resume work, sometimes asking them to be quieter as their brother is sleeping. I could definitely do better by appreciating that my children have things to share with me and try my best to give them my attention. One very useful insight shared by a friend: Resist the urge to ask them about their homework the first thing you see them as they may think that we only care about the work. Ask them about them first!

- **Just before bed.** These are precious moments to wrap up the day, to let the kids go to bed feeling at peace and happy, knowing that they are very loved. The peak-end rule is relevant here: It is about how people tend to judge an experience largely based on how they felt at its peak and at its end, rather than to sum up the experience[3]. This effect occurs regardless of whether the experience was pleasant or unpleasant. As such, we can imagine that if the kids' day went ok but ended badly, they could have thought that it was a bad day overall. Personally, I have always cherished bedtime with the children and we use it as a time for a quick (and sometimes not so quick) catch up filled with lots of cuddles and kisses, especially when the kids were younger. These days, I tend to be quite busy with the baby, but we still try to make time for a quick chat where possible, sharing some laughs before they turn in for the night. The kids also tend to be disappointed if I cannot be with them even for a while, so I would try my best to spend some time with them in bed, even if it were for five minutes.

As they say, the days are long, but the years are short! It may seem like there are countless opportunities to do these things with our kids (three opportunities each day!) but we really wouldn't always be there to start off their day, to welcome them when they are home and to spend them with them before they go to bed. Cherish these precious moments because time flies. Wouldn't you also agree that the above insights apply to adults as well? Because who doesn't want to be woken up gently, to have someone to speak to about their day (who genuinely wants to listen) and to go to bed feeling loved? While we may no longer be as impressionable as kids at these key moments, maybe such moments still matter to adults. See if you can apply the insights to make your kids, as well as your spouse or other loved ones, feel more loved!

---

[1] "Better Parenting (in 9 Minutes a Day)". *Dakota Family Services*, 2 June 2023, www.dakotafamilyservices.org/resources/blog/archive/better-parenting-skills-in-9-minutes-a-day.

[2] "East Framework: Four Simple Ways to Apply Behavioural Insights." *The Behavioural Insights Team*, 7 May 2024, www.bi.team/publications/east-four-simple-ways-to-apply-behavioural-insights/.

[3] "How do our memories differ from our experiences?". *The Decision Lab*, 17 Nov 2023, thedecisionlab.com/biases/peak-end-rule.

Remembering That the Kids Were Once So Small

In behavioural science, there are studies that aim to make people's future selves more salient, to overcome the tendency for people to focus on the present, i.e., the present bias[1]. One such application is in nudging people to plan for their retirement. To say that people are disconnected from their future selves is an understatement. Neurological studies found that our brain activity, when thinking about our future selves, closely resembles that of when we are thinking about other people. As such, people are often not too keen to plan for their retirement at the expense of their present selves because they almost do not see their future selves as themselves!

In 2011, Professor Hal Hershfield of UCLA's Anderson School of Management partnered with Microsoft Research and Stanford's Virtual Human Interaction Lab to see if they could increase the tendency of college-age research subjects planning for their retirement by showing them a retirement-age version of themselves. Some were shown their virtual avatars at age 65, while other subjects saw avatars of their current selves[2]. When asked about their future plans, the amount that the future avatars group said that they were willing to put aside for retirement was about 30 percentage points more than the group that saw their current avatars. The researchers posited that this was due to the Proteus effect, where behavioural modifications in the real world are triggered by changes in how our bodies appear to us virtually. For example, someone who sees his avatar exercising is more likely to do so in real life. In the same vein, research subjects here feel an increased connection with their future selves and tend to be more willing to save more for retirement.

In our scenario though, would it help that we sometimes look back to the past? For those of you who have a photo wall, do you ever reminisce about the days when the children were once small and cute?

The photo wall that keeps growing and growing.

When the going gets tough (e.g., when dealing with the older kids), it may help to remember that they were once so small as well. That when they were very young, like how the new baby is, they could do no wrong. Expectations were a lot lower then. We would be so pleased with a loud burp after a feed, a big smile, a healthy poop colour, etc., while a loud burp in front of others now would probably earn them a chiding. I think it helps to remind ourselves that our expectations have probably increased tenfold or hundredfold, just because they have surpassed those adorable baby and toddler years, and that when they were small, we would have never thought of screaming at them or speaking harshly to them.

I think looking back at the past can sometimes
help us to cut the kids some slack and carry on in
a calmer and more loving manner. They are, after all,
still the same people, just older and perhaps just slightly
more assertive. Looking at that family photo wall
in difficult times may help!

---

[1] "Present Bias – Everything You Need to Know". *insideBE*, 19 Dec 2023, insidebe.com/articles/present-bias/.

[2] "You Make Better Decisions If You "See" Your Future Self". *Harvard Business Review*, 10 Apr 2022, hbr.org/2013/06/you-make-better-decisions-if-you-see-your-senior-self.

Motivating Good Studying Behaviour and Inculcating a Habit

What many parents may be interested in is how we can motivate good studying behaviour among the children? Further to motivating them, how can we also help to build a good studying habit?

Motivation is defined as one's route that leads to behaviour, or what triggers the desire to replicate behaviour. Motivation is not fixed. It is better represented on a scale where one's attitude towards a particular behaviour can range from being amotivated (unmotivated) to being extrinsically motivated (driven by external factors), to being intrinsically motivated (doing something because one enjoys it and not because of external factors).

An important theory in motivation is the Self-Determination Theory, developed by psychologists Edward Deci and Richard Ryan. The theory explores why being self-determined towards adopting a certain behaviour is important for motivation and how we can bring about self-determination[1]. As the name suggests, self-determination means wanting and having the intrinsic motivation to do something. One may have the resolve if he or she made the choice to do it and is also able to. The theory thus suggests that people can become self-determined towards adopting a behaviour when their needs for competence, relatedness and autonomy are met:

- **Competence.** When people feel competent about doing something, they are more likely to be intrinsically motivated to do it. Ways to foster a sense of competence towards a task include providing positive feedback, making progress salient, providing rewards for completing challenges or by increasing the level of challenges.
- **Relatedness.** People are more motivated to do something when others are also doing it and when there is some sort of comparison. Ways to increase relatedness include finding communities that pursue the same activity, e.g., a special interest group, as well as the use of leader boards and social comparisons among peer groups.
- **Autonomy.** Not surprisingly, people would also be more motivated to do something if they were able to decide whether they want to do it and if so, when and how.

Tackling the motivation part first, how can we nudge the children towards being self-determined or intrinsically motivated to do their revision—or at the very least, lean more towards the right of the scale? I employed a mix of the above factors:

- **Competence.** For their exam revision, each child has a progress chart that is affixed to the wall so that their progress is visible to all. They get a positive feedback sticker for good studying behaviour for the day and earn a sure-win lucky dip from the "Good

Studying Behaviour" rewards box (for snacks or other goodies) for every three stickers earned.

- **Relatedness.** While I did not use a leaderboard since there are only two of them, putting the charts side by side does provide some form of social comparison. Neither kid wants to lose out to the other, so they try their best to earn their daily stickers. They are both also pursuing the same goal, so there is perceived fairness and a sense that they both have to do this. It may feel quite different if only one out of two children was asked to study.

- **Autonomy.** Studying is a must during exam period, but where there is no stipulated revision for the day, the kids could choose to self-study to earn their stickers, which they did because they really wanted to earn the reward!

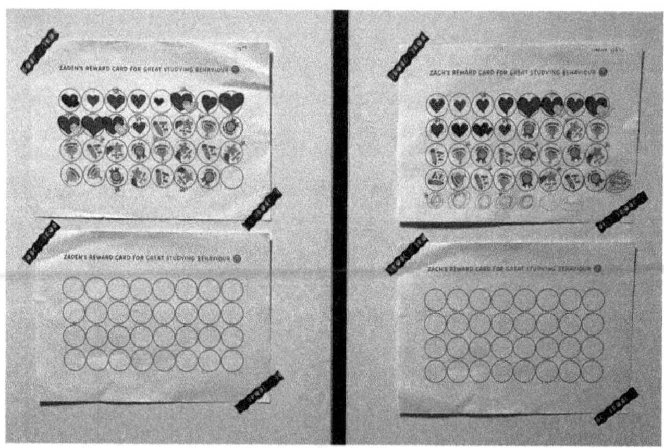

The progress charts.

What we did was also a manifestation of the Hooked Model for habit formation by Nir Eyal, which involves the steps, Trigger, Action, Variable Rewards and Investment (after which hopefully, the cycle repeats)[2]. For instance, the trigger is a new day on the progress chart, the action is to study well for the day, the variable reward is the lucky dip for every three stickers earned and investment refers to the child investing more time and effort to study well when he is convinced that doing so leads to fulfilling rewards, thereby resulting in habit formation!

A Quick Word About Extrinsic Motivation

You may also have noticed that while I employed the Self-Determination Theory to inculcate intrinsic motivation among the kids to study well, one key motivator (the rewards) in my approach is really quite extrinsic in nature. Although we always aim for intrinsic motivation in getting people to do something, there is also a school of thought that it is possible to start with extrinsic motivation because once the desired behaviour becomes a habit, it could still continue even with the removal of the rewards. We should, however, be quite cautious about employing extrinsic motivation to nudge pro-social behaviours. For example, it would not be appropriate to provide people with a monetary reward for donating blood as it can crowd out the intrinsic motivation for doing so by shifting the meaning behind donating blood from altruism to one of personal gain. Doing so may also lead to ethical concerns. Similarly, we do not want to use external rewards to motivate our children to be respectful to the elders or to be kind to animals, for example.

The above strategy worked quite well for their last exam revision and I am quite keen to revive it again. I found it to be quite effective because even the younger one, who's really quite chill, kept asking for work so that he could earn his sticker. They were also rather disappointed when I paused the "programme" after the exams (mainly because it was getting too tiring to stock up on the goodies and they were having too many snacks, an unintended consequence from my intervention!). Nevertheless, I would be most willing to do it for specific periods requiring more discipline and motivation, like during the exam period.

Pushing it further, is it possible to make good studying behaviour automatic to the children on a daily basis? The Fogg Behaviour Model could be relevant here. It posits that for someone to perform a behaviour continually, the person should be sufficiently motivated; he or she must have the ability to perform the action; and triggers or prompts must be well-timed for action[3]. Assuming that I have earlier trained my children well, and that they are sufficiently motivated and know what I mean by good studying behaviour or knowing what to do, I may be able to replicate the desired behaviour by designing effective prompts that trigger the desired action. For example, a signal that the younger one should start his work—an alarm that goes off every day at 3 p.m.—which should be appropriately-timed so it allows him enough time for lunch and a not-too-short mental break before he commences his work.

The research on motivation and habit formation is really interesting and applicable to a wide range of behaviours that we may want to bring about in our children, beyond study matters. It is worth reading up and experimenting to find out which approach works best for your children.

[1] Deci, Edward L., and Richard M. Ryan. "Self-determination theory." *Handbook of Theories of Social Psychology: Volume 1*, 2012, pp. 416–437, doi.org/10.4135/9781446249215.n21.

[2] "The Hooked Model: How to Manufacture Desire in 4 Steps". *Nir And Far*, 3 Mar 2023, www.nirandfar.com/how-to-manufacture-desire/#:~:text=The%20cycle%20in%20the%20Hooked,has%20more%20value%20to%20him.

[3] "Fogg Behavior Model". *Stanford Behavior Design Lab*, 5 Sep 2022, behaviordesign.stanford.edu/resources/fogg-behavior-model.

The Dreaded "Pump and Dump"

For those of you who are on a breastfeeding journey with your new baby, "pump and dump" should be one of those horrors that you would not wish upon any breastfeeding mothers. It essentially refers to the pumping and then discarding of milk, usually for a period of time, especially when you are taking certain medications that may enter the breastmilk and pose risks to the baby. Pumping and dumping is hard because you may be next to the baby, but you are unable to feed him or her. It is also hard work that literally has to go down the drain. But what if there is really no choice at all?

I first experienced pumping and dumping many years ago when I was nursing my second son. Having to travel for work two weeks after returning from my maternity leave, I had to pump and dump as it was difficult to store the breastmilk (I travelled to the US for more than a week). It was challenging to find opportunities to express breastmilk on a work trip because there were no proper rooms that I could easily find, there was only the toilet and to say that pumping on the plane was a pain is an understatement. By the time I returned, owing to the poor pumping routine, my supply was almost non-existent. I had to work triply hard to restart the feeding, which fortunately got better after a while.

Unfortunately, the second time round, I had to pump and dump as I had a bad skin flare-up and needed to take steroid medications. As I had to finish the course of medicine over four days, my doctor advised pumping and dumping for four plus another three days to ensure that the medicines are flushed out of my system. He explained that steroids may impact babies' growth. This meant seven long days of not being able to nurse! It was upsetting. but it was also not something that could be helped. As my husband rightly pointed out, "He is an infant and we cannot allow him to ingest the steroids, no matter how little the amount. If the milk is not beneficial, we should not feed it." This helped to put my thoughts into perspective and reminded me why we wanted to nurse him in the first place.

I thought I'd share some tips on how you could get through this if you unfortunately find yourself in a similar predicament:

- I had a bad skin flare-up that I put up with for more than two months. I had in fact seen the doctor at the onset, but I was not willing to pump and dump. I could not imagine doing it just to take the medication. It almost felt as if it was not worth it. I said that I will bear with it and see how it goes. On reflection, I was present biased by putting more weight on the here and now (i.e., the nursing) and neglecting the longer term (i.e., getting well). I did not realise it then that it would be better to grin and bear it, and restart nursing when I am better. On hindsight, I should have done it when I first saw the doctor and would probably have recovered soon after.

- I also did not prioritise self-care when I made the decision to delay treatment. I forgot that to be able to give the best care to my baby, I needed to be physically and mentally well. The condition affected me physically, but it also caused me a lot of distress!

- We can try to find some ways to make the waiting more bearable. Research shows that people find it easier to wait when they know how long they have to wait for, as there is certainty[1]. It might also help to provide a sense of progress that the wait is getting shorter. In a sense, this is similar to the Goal Gradient Effect where the hypothesis is that people feel increased motivation towards achieving a goal as they get closer to it. (Recall how you may have purchased more bubble tea as you got closer to accumulating 10 stamps to earn the reward[2].) Here, we might feel increased relief that the wait is going to be over, giving us the resolve to press on. I used a simple calendar countdown to strike the days off daily and felt comfort as we approached the end of the challenging wait.

- Some reframing may also be helpful here. Try to think of the good side. This episode gave me a lot of experience in pumping and provided me with the confidence that I would be able to continue pumping successfully when I am back at work. I was also able to sneak in an extra coffee when I needed it since it would not impact the feeding.

Challenging as it seems, it always helps to find
the good even in a seemingly bad situation.
Remember that it is always possible to do so because
there is more than one side and perspective to things.
We just have to look harder.

---

[1] "The Psychology of Waiting: 8 Factors that Make the Wait Seem Longer". *PsychCentral*, 20 Jan 2023, psychcentral.com/blog/the-psychology-of-waiting-in-lines-8-reasons-that-the-wait-seems-long#1.

[2] Hull, C. L. "The goal-gradient hypothesis and maze learning." *Psychological Review*, vol. 39, no. 1, Jan. 1932, pp. 25–43, doi.org/10.1037/h0072640.

Keeping the House Tidy With the Broken Windows Theory

In criminology, the Broken Windows Theory, proposed by social scientists James Q. Wilson and George L. Kelling, suggests that visible signs of disorder, such as vandalism, loitering and broken windows signal that an area is neglected, inviting more disorder and crime[1]. Wilson and Kelling argued that addressing such behaviour, e.g., through cleaning up graffiti, increasing policing and repairing broken windows, allows an area to appear to be more cared for or protected, thus reducing crime.

However, the theory is a controversial one. Critics highlight that there is limited evidence to suggest that a clear, causal relationship exists between disorder in an environment and crime. Some were also of the view that the theory can be used to justify over-policing of certain communities, such as the low-income and minority communities, propagating bias.

Putting the criticisms surrounding the Broken Windows Theory aside, can there be room for applying the theory in the home? Can it also be the case that homes, once left messy and disorganised for an extended period of time, just become messier?

This thought came to my mind when I observed how the kids (and also myself) behaved. When I did not make my bed in the morning, there was a tendency for the kids to pounce on it and chill in bed for an extended period of time. They said that this is because Mummy's bed is so comfortable! When the bed is tidy, however, this rarely happens. Reflecting also on my own behaviour, I tend to want to keep neat spaces neat, while keeping one eye (or both) closed on the very messy areas. This may not entirely gel with the concept of the Broken Windows Theory, but there are similarities in that when spaces are not upkept, they seem to get messier and sprucing up becomes even more difficult.

This is just food for thought because we know our homes will only get messier and more cluttered with a new baby! Small as they are, babies seem to have an unfathomable amount of clothes, wash cloths, lotions, bottles, diapers, toys and more!

When things have stabilised somewhat and we feel slightly more on top of things, maybe we can start tidying up parts of the home we feel more strongly about. For example, if you are like me and like the bed to be kept neat and clean (my mother taught us never to go to the bed without taking a bath), you may want to make your bed first thing in the morning!

---

[1] "Broken Windows Theory". *Psychology Today*, 30 May 2023, https://www. psychologytoday.com/sg/basics/broken-windows-theory?amp

Case
Studies:
Real-life
Applications

This section consists of a small collection of case studies where behavioural science is applied in the personal lives of my teammates "Jelly", Hazel, James and Stephen. The case studies are roughly structured according to the behavioural target(s) and behavioural science application(s), and in each, a short explanation of the concepts involved is given.

Case Study 1: "Jelly", Nudging My Nephew and Niece

I like to leverage insights from behavioural science to encourage my nephew to learn his ABCs or use his fine motor skills. This is to encourage him to take up tasks that he deems to be difficult or beyond his ability. I will usually try to make things easy and attractive for him.

Examples:

- Before teaching him his ABCs, I will start my lesson with a video (that sings the letter sound and shows things that start with that alphabet) because he likes to sing and it is also easier to remember with a song.
- Using lots of encouragement like praises and star stickers.
- Helping him anticipate success by asking him, "After you finish writing this, who would you like to show your achievement to?"
- Breaking things down into simpler steps, e.g., asking him to find a particular picture in letter puzzles.

I also use substitution at home to influence the kids' behaviour. They are told that they cannot climb on the sofa and bed, but they can climb on the balance stepping stones that I bought for them instead.

Concept: Self-determination theory + Behavioural substitution

Recall that the Self-determination Theory posits that when people feel competent towards undertaking a task, they are more likely to be intrinsically motivated to do it. Much of what Jelly is doing is to instil a sense of capability and confidence in her nephew that he will be able to do the said tasks. When we want people to do something, it is indeed important to consider whether it is easy for them to do so and whether the request can be made more attractive, e.g., by making the benefits of doing so salient. Jelly has "made it easy" for her nephew by going with the grain of how he likes to learn (through song videos) and also considering how to break down his learning tasks into simpler steps for him (for the puzzles). Helping him to anticipate success and thinking whom to share his success with is indeed a very clever way of making the benefits of studying well salient!

Behavioural substitution refers to the replacement of problematic behaviours with acceptable ones, often involving substituted behaviours that have similar sensory qualities as the original one. Here, Jelly has provided balance stepping stones to allow her nephew and niece to climb where it is allowed. It is indeed a behaviourally-informed strategy by a wonderful aunt!

Case Study 2: Hazel, Nudging My Daughter Tasha

To nudge my daughter Tasha to undertake the following behaviours willingly:

- When it's bedtime I ask, "Do you want Mummy to put you to bed or Auntie Siti?"
- When it's mealtime I ask, "Which spoon do you want to use?"
- When it's time for school I ask, "Do you want one ponytail or two?"

Concept: Self-determination theory + Zone of proximal development

We know that people would be more motivated to do something if they were able to decide whether they want to do it and if so, when and how. Here, while Hazel certainly wants her daughter to go to bed, eat her meal and get ready for school, instead of instructing her to do so, she has provided her with choices related to the desired behaviour to nudge compliance while providing a sense of autonomy. Very clever!

Hazel is also trying to encourage Tasha to use the shower head instead of the bathtub at bathtimes (Tasha is afraid of, but also curious about the shower head). She will get Tasha to wash her hands first, followed by the feet, then up to the knees, the waist, etc., and if she is able to manage with using the shower head above the shoulders, she gets rewarded with lots of praise and affirmation from Mummy.

Gleaning from Vgotsky's Zone of Proximal Development, a prominent theory in developmental psychology about challenging learners at an optimal level (i.e., the gap between actual and potential development) and calibrating tasks to the learner's level with the appropriate guidance and support so they can be completed successfully, Hazel carefully notices Tasha's progress and adjusts the task to help her overcome her fear of shower heads. Tasha was not afraid of washing her hands and was open to washing her feet. These multiple mini moments of success build Tasha's confidence in accomplishing the task. Hazel was able to help Tasha wash her body with the showerhead a few times. She is sure that Tasha will eventually be able to wash her hair with the showerhead and to do it by herself!

Update at the time of print: Tasha progressed to allowing Hazel to wash her hair while she stands and looks up! She is still wary of the shower head because the spray is strong and water gets on her face, but is okay with Hazel using a water scoop. Hazel tried to reduce her anxiety by increasing certainty. She promised Tasha that she only needed to look up for five counts each time. She would emphasise how brave Tasha was for trying and reinforce that nothing bad happened. There were also a few occasions at the swimming pool where Tasha saw her fellow toddlers getting their hair "washed" and enjoying it.

Case Study 3: James, Various Strategies to Nudge My Son Kyan

I have tried the following to encourage Kyan to pick up good character traits and good habits:

- Highlight positive social norms. If I see his favourite character in the show doing something positive, I will highlight it to him and ask what he thinks the character has done and how it made others feel. I will also explain why I felt that the behaviour is positive and encourage him to practise it in future.

- Role modelling (related to the above point). I would also tell him that if he wants to be like the character in his favourite show, he can try practising the good traits and behaviours shown. For example, taking deep breaths to calm down when he is angry (from the show "Daniel Tiger").

- Making progress salient. When Kyan is stuck in his homework and finds it difficult to continue, I will encourage him to see the progress he has already made and to continue trying. Every time he progresses, I will provide positive feedback to encourage him and help him feel competent.

- Use of a "roadmap" to help Kyan learn his routines, i.e., having a visual chart to show what he needs to do from dinnertime to washing up, to bedtime.

Kyan's roadmap.

Concept: Self-determination theory + Goal gradient hypothesis + Social norms

We see Competence from the Self-determination Theory as James tries to instil a sense of competency by providing positive feedback, making Kyan's progress salient. He also taps on the goal gradient hypothesis to encourage Kyan to work harder to complete his work. James has also applied what we call descriptive social norms by providing information on what others do—in this case, positive behaviour exhibited by Kyan's favourite character in the show. Social norms are powerful because people are very much influenced by others, and they want to blend in and be accepted. Norms have also been found to be more effective when people are told that their peers or "people like them" have exhibited a certain behaviour, as there is greater relevance. In this case, James has tapped on Kyan's favourite characters to communicate the positive social norm and role model—you can imagine how effective that would be!

The roadmap helps Kyan visualise and better understand what is required of him at various timepoints of the day and also serves as a timely reminder on what to do next.

Case Study 4: Stephen, Many Applications of Behavioural Science in My Life

- Managing my children: I tell them, "Most children at your age should be able to [do this action]," to nudge them to undertake a certain behaviour. However, I will not mention names to avoid unhealthy comparisons.
- Managing my subscriptions: One of my favourites! The moment I sign up for a free subscription, I will set a few reminders on my phone so that I will remember to cancel the subscriptions.
- Securing commitment for meetups: When arranging meetups with people, I will fix the dates with them on the spot if possible. This is so that they will commit to the meet-up.
- For business trips or family vacations: So that I do not forget to bring my essentials, I created a checklist on my iPhone Notes using the checklist function. I will use the same checklist every time I am packing for trips to reduce the number of things I forget to bring. If I indeed forget to bring something, I will add the item into the checklist for future reference.

Concept: Social norms + reminders + commitment mechanisms

Like James, Stephen uses social norms to manage his children. However, he uses injunctive instead of descriptive norms, which refers to communicating what people *should* do rather than informing what they have done. Injunctive norms can be very useful when we do not actually have a positive social norm to highlight.

The reminders to cancel the free subscriptions are indeed very helpful. We all know how easy it is to miss the deadline for cancelling such subscriptions before they automatically roll over: Payment is enforced and it is not possible to get a refund. Salient, timely reminders should help! Another form of reminders, checklists are extremely useful as a memory aid, promoting consistency and also providing peace of mind and assurance that important things will not be overlooked.

Finally, what Stephen is doing by securing commitments to meetups is really to bridge the intention-action gap that we earlier talked about! To narrow such a gap, an effective measure has indeed been to get people to commit to doing something and it is more effective when done on the spot. In general, public commitments are more effective than commitments made in private. This is because nobody knows if you go back on your word if you made the commitment privately whereas in person, people feel greater pressure to stick to their commitments because they like to think of themselves as being consistent.

What Kids Think and Feel: Insights by a Pre-teen

Hi, I'm Zachary, 12, and I will be writing this special section of *New Baby, New Life* so you parents can have an idea of what we kids think and feel!

Things that make us kids, written by the 11-year-old me 😊:

- **Kids like attention.** Spend some time chatting with your kids sometimes and asking them about their day. Tip: If you ask and they won't open up to you, try asking again while walking because they will be distracted and may not notice that they are telling you about their day. If this does not work, wait a while for them to forget before asking again or they may snap.

- **Acknowledge your kids for the things that they do.** When your child does something good, they will expect you to say something along the lines of "good job" or "very good". If you don't, they will feel like they've been ignored and they will be sad.

- **Kids like rewards.** Possible rewards they will appreciate include toys, games or extra play time.

- **Need for independence.** Kids will want to be more independent when they reach 10. This may be because they are influenced by their friends who enjoy more freedom. You should establish an agreement, e.g., to allow your kids to go out once or twice in a while instead of not at all.

- **Too much invasion of privacy.** Kids will want a bit of privacy, e.g., with regard to who they are talking to or what they are doing. Avoid insensitive topics and going too far in detail about what your child is doing.

Things that make us kids, written by the 12-year-old me 😊:

- **Firstly, what you see may not be what immediately comes to mind.** Should you catch your child in what looks like an act of misbehaving, do not be so quick to assume because as a wise person (i.e., my father) once said, "To assume is making an ass out of u and me."

- **Secondly, your child may be more tempted to go out more.** Speaking from experience, we kids want to keep up with the times and grow our own social life.

- **Lastly, privacy is important.** (This point has been stressed on earlier.) As much as parents want to know or check what's up with their child, unbeknownst to most parents, privacy is important to kids too. Kids may feel scared to socialise with their friends over text for fear of parents reading their messages (like some of my friends) which prevent them from being able to happily forge memories from the wonders of online chats. Parents shouldn't check children's phones without their knowledge because it may cause them to lose their trust in you. They may also start to keep more stuff from you.

That is all for my section. I hope you are able to understand your kids better now! Thank you for reading!

Zachary

How interesting it is to gain insight to our child's mind! For those of you who have an older child like mine, you can consider asking him or her to pen his or her thoughts on pointers that you can note to ensure their happiness or sanity. This is also quite related to the segment on speaking to our kids in their love languages. Besides that, we also need to be aware of what's important to them and whether they have any feedback to share!

Afterword

Hello again! I'm stoked that you have read the book cover to cover—well, almost! You can probably imagine that writing a book isn't easy, not only because of the research and writing involved, but perhaps also the questions that authors may have for themselves (Do I really want to do this? Is what I am writing about worth reading?).

Indeed, my biggest hope for this book is that it is worth reading and that as you were flipping through the pages, parts of it resonated with you, you found some parts interesting because they were new or surprising information, and perhaps you even felt that you gleaned something useful from some parts. Only then, the nights, weekends and years I spent on this book would not have been in vain. Admittedly, I also wrote this book for my children, in the hope that they can one day find it useful (future thinking!), and yes, it is more to record the current moment in time where we are all still very much together, for the times ahead when we may not be for one reason or another.

This book also brings together two areas that I feel very strongly about: Firstly, knowing how to be happy in everyday life because every day may not always be exciting and packed with good things, and we do need to know how to be contented with the smaller things to be generally happy and satisfied with our lives. Secondly, the portion on behavioural science applied to personal life is a culmination of the knowledge I have gained in this area through the years. Its application in our daily life is an aspect not so much explored in the current behavioural insights literature. I do hope that you will find both segments relevant and useful for you!

As you may already know from reading this book, reading about something useful is one thing and making effort to do something differently is another! My behaviourally-informed appeal to you would be to consider, if you agreed with some parts of this book how you can do something differently and to make a plan for it. Think about:

- What can you do differently to make your life with your new baby a smoother and more enjoyable one?
- How do you plan to make this change?
- Can it be incorporated into your routine so that there is a higher chance of applying the behaviour?

Planning is an important part of making changes. Research on goal pursuit tells us that drafting concrete plans makes us more likely to follow through our intentions. When tasks are scheduled, we are more likely to carry them out as we have planned to make time for them. The action of writing them down also serves as a form of commitment to ourselves. You may or may not be able to follow the plan every day, but it should be easier than if there were no plan.

One idea that you could consider is to have a daily plan to incorporate some form of well-being in your life. I did this during my maternity leave! See examples of how such a plan can look like (e.g., mine) with a to-do list inspired by bullet journalling that you can easily make every day. I have also included a "Grateful for" list to make a record of events and things that I appreciate and do not want to take for granted, as a daily reminder of the positive things that are happening in my life. In this daily list, you can plan to do something that brings you joy, as discussed in the joyspotting strategy in Part 1 of the book.

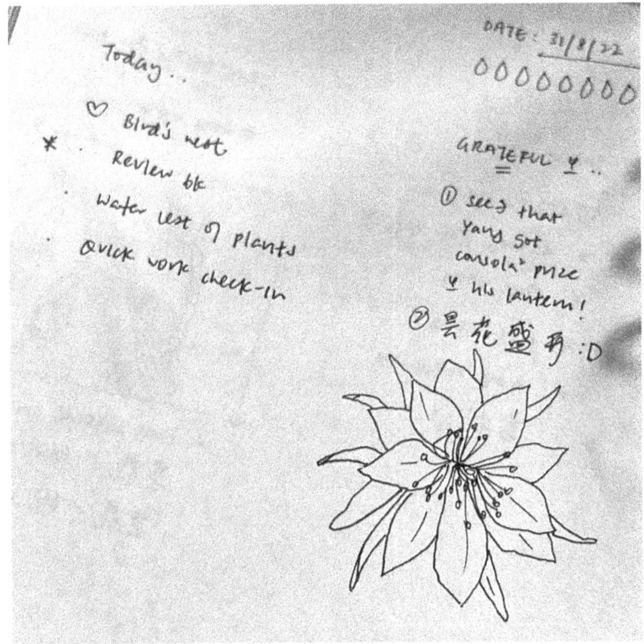

My daily plan in the form of bullet journalling.

Again, thank you very much for spending time to read *New Baby, New Life*. I do wish you the very best and I hope that this book can help to make your life happier and easier. I'd love to hear your opinions on the book and your experiences after trying out the tips! You can reach me at newbabynewlife.book@gmail.com or my Instagram account at @newbabynewlife_book.

Hope to hear from you and take good care!

About the Author

Sabrina Ng is a public servant from Singapore, who has clocked 20 years of service, of which a large part was spent on research in Behavioural Insights (BI) and its application to improve the government's work and in building BI capability. She has a Bachelor of Science in Computing from the National University of Singapore and a Masters in Behavioural Science from the London School of Economics and Political Science, for which she won the "To Know the Causes of Things" prize for best dissertation in her cohort. Sabrina is also the proud mother of the Z Bros (Zachary, Zaden and Zander), without whom this book would not have been written.